GENETIC MODIFICATION

Should Humans Control Nature?

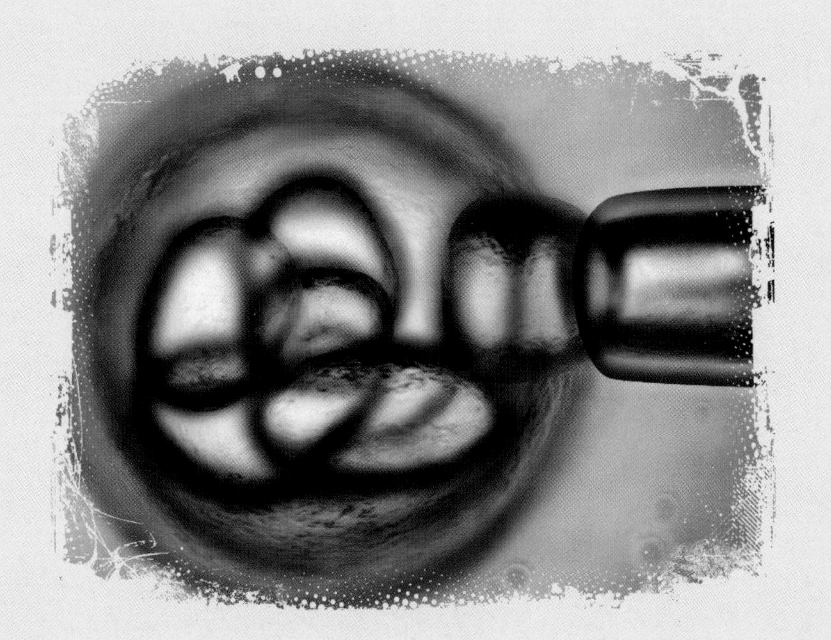

Leon Gray

Please visit our website, www.garethstevens.com. For a free color catalog of all our high-quality books, call toll free 1-800-542-2595 or fax 1-877-542-2596.

Publisher Cataloging Data

Gray, Leon, 1974-
Genetic modification : should humans control nature? / Leon Gray.
p. cm. – (Ask the experts)
Summary: This book explains how genetic modification, or GM, is being used today and challenges the reader to form their own opinion as to whether GM is right or wrong.
Contents: In the genes – Inside a gene – Cloning – Genetic modification – GM in action – GM in food – GM medicine – Science and industry – You're the expert.
ISBN 978-1-4339-8635-2 (hard bound) – ISBN 978-1-4339-8636-9 (pbk.)
ISBN 978-1-4339-8637-6 (6-pack)
1. Recombinant DNA—Research—Moral and ethical aspects—Juvenile literature 2.Genomics—Moral and ethical aspects—Juvenile literature 3. Genetic engineering—Moral and ethical aspects –Juvenile literature [1. Genetic engineering] I. Title
QH442.G729 2013
660.6/5—dc23 2012037836

First Edition

Published in 2013 by
Gareth Stevens Publishing
111 East 14th Street, Suite 349
New York, NY 10003

Produced by Calcium, www.calciumcreative.co.uk
Designed by Emma DeBanks and Paul Myerscough
Edited by Sarah Eason

Photo credits: Shutterstock: Galyna Andrushko 30, AnetaPics 14, Andrey Armyagov 8, Auremar 39, Jason Bennee 5, Dmitrijs Bindemanis 11, Blend Images 42t, Bluehand 20, CURAphotography 37, Robert Davies 6, Lev Dolgachov 38, Charlie Edward 31, EGD 41, Elena Elisseeva 12, Paul Fleet 1, 17, Fotocrisis 7, Goodluz 13, Jubal Harshaw 34, Homeros 27, 45, Tischenko Irina 15, Marcel Jancovic 19, Sebastian Kaulitzki 44, Lculig 22, 36, Dmitry Lobanov 35, Joe Mercier 9, Michelangelus 24, Mycola 26, Negative cover (bg), Nobeastsofierce 25, Sura Nualpradid 32, Alexander Raths 43b, Lisa S. 42, Pedro Salaverría 21, Manuel Schafer 33, Stephen Snyder 29, Murat Subatli 40, TaXZi 3, 28, Tish1 18, VGM 16, Wavebreakmedia ltd 10, 23, Lawrence Wee 4, Monika Wisniewska cover (fg).

Printed in the United States of America

CPSIA compliance information: Batch #CW13GS: For further information contact Gareth Stevens, New York, New York at 1-800-542-2595.

Contents

Did you know that most of the healthy cells in your body each contain around 35,000 genes? Genes are the tiny pieces of information that determine how your body looks and works. Genes are found inside almost every cell.

In the Genes

Scientists have carried out many experiments to try to figure out what genes do and how they work. They know that genes pass from parents to their children. The young of some living things are identical copies of one parent, called clones. In others, the genes from both parents combine to produce offspring with similar, but not identical, features.

"the debate

Genetic modification has become a hot topic for debate among scientists, politicians, and the public. Some people think this modern science will help us deal with the global problems of disease and famine. Others disagree. They say the effects of genetic engineering on the environment and on public health make it dangerous."

Scientists grow plant clones in the laboratory to create crops that are resistant to pests and diseases.

Experiments with GM have produced genetically identical animals such as sheep.

Genetic Modification

Genetic modification (GM) is the scientific experimentation with genes to change the way a living thing looks and behaves. Scientists change genes for different reasons. They have used GM to create crops that stay fresh for longer. GM also helps scientists to produce medicines that can be used to fight diseases, such as cancer.

Who Is Right?

Should scientists take nature into their own hands? Is genetic modification improving our lives, or could it be putting us in danger? In this book, we ask the experts for answers to these questions. We'll then ask you to become the expert and make up your own mind about whether GM is right or wrong.

Face Facts

"With the tools and the knowledge, I could turn a developing snail's egg into an elephant. It is not so much a matter of chemicals, because snails and elephants do not differ that much; it is a matter of timing the action of genes."
Barbara McClintock, Nobel Prize-winning botanist

In the 1860s, an Austrian scientist named Gregor Mendel conducted experiments with pea plants. Mendel bred plants with different physical traits, such as height or flower color. He realized that each trait came about because of a "unit" passed on to each plant from each of its parents. Scientists called these "units" genes.

Inside a Gene

Around the same time as Mendel was experimenting with pea plants, a Swiss scientist named Friedrich Miescher found a substance called DNA inside human cells. DNA stands for deoxyribonucleic acid. Over time, scientists realized there was a link between DNA and genes. Scientists wanted to learn more about genes, but first they needed to work out the structure of DNA.

Face Facts

"DNA is like a computer program but far, far more advanced than any software ever created."
Bill Gates, Founder of Microsoft Corporation, in *The Road Ahead* (1995)

This plant cell contains DNA. Scientists extract DNA to find out more about the different traits of the plant.

Twisted Ladder

In 1953, the scientists Francis Crick and James Watson figured out the structure of DNA. They discovered that, up close, DNA looks like a twisted ladder. Two strands of sugars and other molecules make up the upright poles of the DNA ladder. The rungs of the ladder between the poles are pairs of chemicals called "bases."

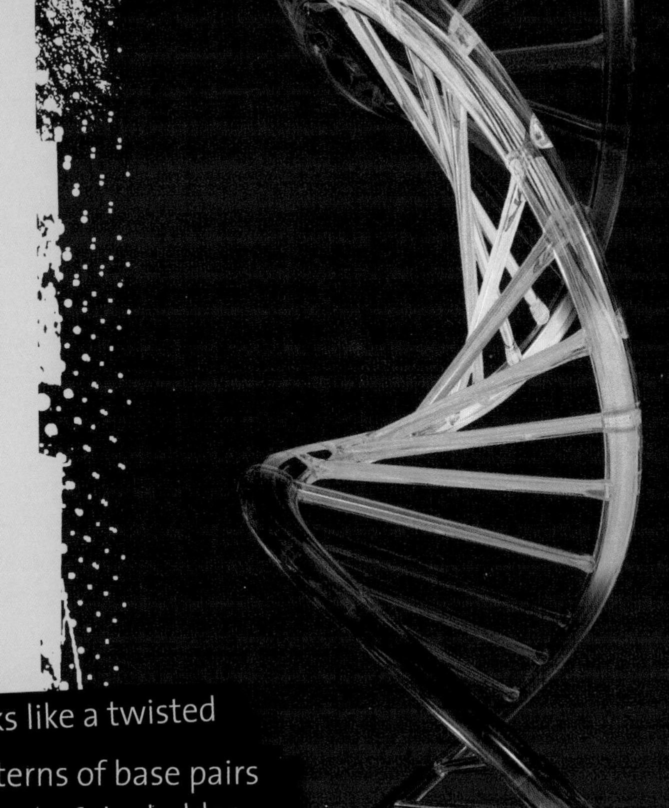

Under a microscope, DNA looks like a twisted ladder. Genes are the patterns of base pairs that make up the rungs of the ladder.

"the debate

Crick and Watson took most of the credit for figuring out the structure of DNA. Another scientist, Rosalind Franklin, did not get the recognition she deserved. Franklin took detailed images of the DNA molecule that helped Crick and Watson work out its structure. Many people think that Franklin was ignored because she was a female scientist, working in a field of science that is dominated by men."

Pairing Bases

DNA has four bases. Each one has a name, but it is usually written as a letter: A, C, G, and T. A and T always pair up, and G and C always pair up. Genes are patterns of these pairings along the DNA ladder. Different genes tell the cells in your body what to do.

Instructions in Genes

If you could unzip a molecule of DNA and read the patterns of bases along the ladder, you would see a long series of letters, like this: -AGAATCCAGGACTTAATC-. This may look like garbled nonsense, but it contains instructions that a cell can understand. So, how does this work?

DNA Alphabet

The four bases are the "alphabet" of genes. They spell out "words" that are always three bases long: -AGA-ATC-CAG-GAC-TTA-ATC-. In turn, these three-letter words spell out "sentences." These sentences are the genes that tell your body how to work. They do this by telling your cells to make proteins. Proteins control all the different life processes that go on inside your body.

Face Facts

"We are here to celebrate the completion of the first survey of the entire human genome. Without a doubt, this is the most important, most wondrous map ever produced by humankind." President Bill Clinton, White House address, June 26, 2000

Genes control everything about you—even the color of your eyes.

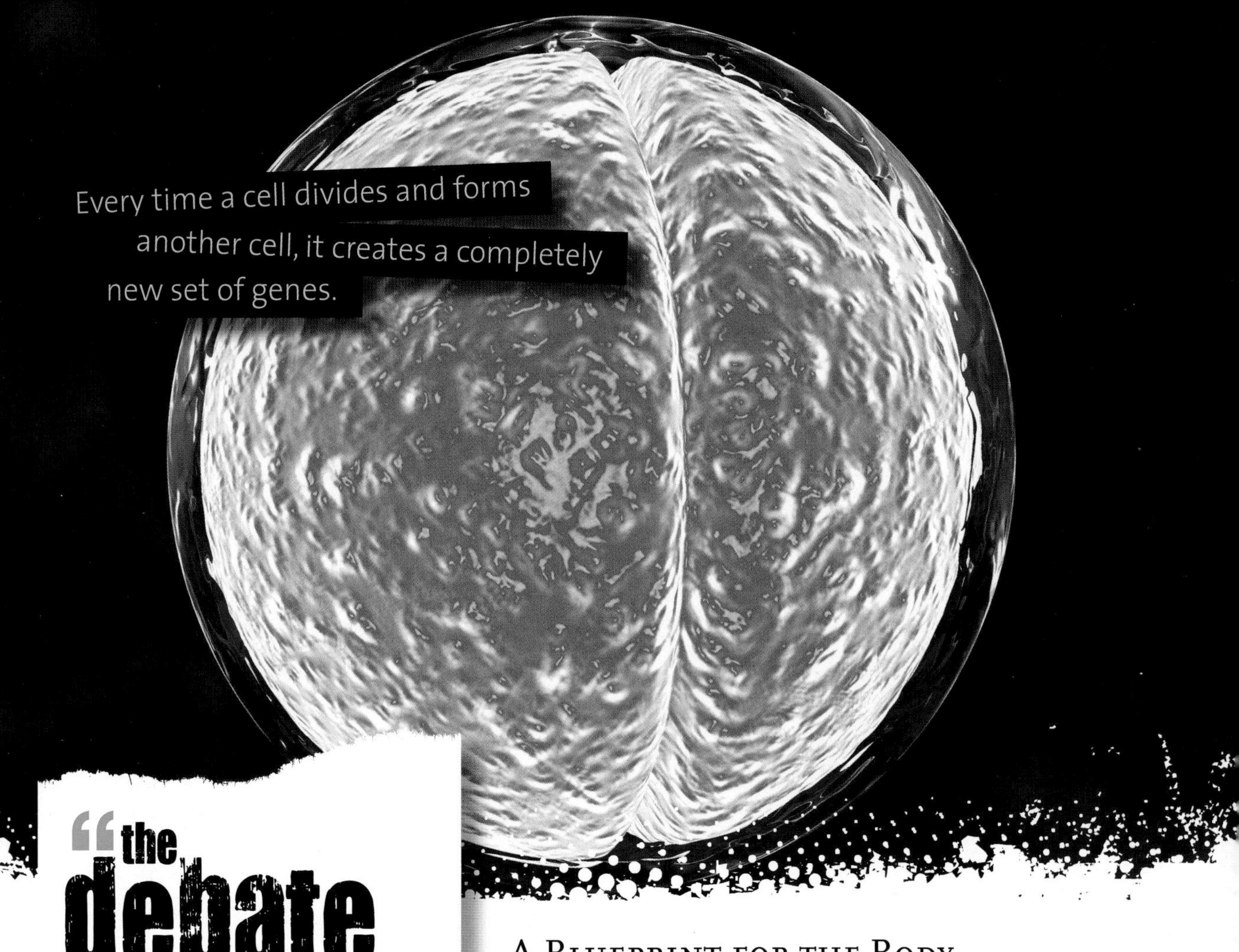

Every time a cell divides and forms another cell, it creates a completely new set of genes.

“the debate”

So far, scientists have identified around 35,000 human genes. Some cause diseases, such as some forms of cancer. Doctors can now study the DNA in your cells to see if you are likely to develop these diseases. The question is, is it right to tell people they could one day die from a terrible disease?

A Blueprint for the Body

Almost every cell in your body contains all the genes that make you who you are. This complete set of genes is called your genome. The human genome is the blueprint for your body. It controls what color eyes you have, how tall you are, and whether you have straight, wavy, or curly hair.

Human Genome Project

In 1990, scientists started the Human Genome Project. They wanted to map the entire pattern of bases in human DNA—all 3 billion of them! The project took 10 years to complete. Scientists published the human genome on the Internet, so that everyone would have access to it. They are now studying patterns of human DNA to find all the different genes in the human genome.

Children inherit features that are similar to those of their parents, such as dark hair.

“the debate

Genes can tell you if you got green eyes from your mother and blonde hair from your father. But what makes you a risk taker, or a talented musician? Do we learn these things during our childhood, or are they written in our genes? Expert opinion is divided over whether “nature” or “nuture” creates personality.”

Passing on Genes

Have you ever wondered why you might look like your parents? The answer lies in your genes. Scientists know that genes are the patterns of DNA. These genes make you who you are. Scientists also know that genes pass down the generations, from parents to their children. So, if a child has blue eyes and red hair, people in their family, either their parents, grandparents, or even great-grandparents, must have had red hair or blue eyes, too.

Chromosomes

The DNA inside cells is wrapped up to form structures called chromosomes. Most cells in the human body contain 23 pairs of chromosomes, making a total of 46. Each pair of chromosomes contains one set of genes from your mother and one set from your father. The genes combine during sexual reproduction, when a male sperm cell joins with a female egg cell and fertilizes it.

Controlled by Genes

Different genes control different characteristics. One gene may control eye color. Another may control height. If both your parents have blonde hair, the chances are that you will be blonde, too. Sometimes this does not work and parents with blonde hair have a child with dark hair. Why does this happen?

Gene Pairs

Every person carries two genes for each characteristic—one from the mother's egg and one from the father's sperm. The different forms of the same gene are called "alleles." One of the alleles will be dominant over the other. In the gene that controls height, the "tall" allele will always dominate the "short" one. This explains why a tall father and short mother will have tall children.

Face Facts

"This is the basis of sexual reproduction—the ability of chromosomes to pair up and divide."
Professor Abby Dernburg, UCLA, Berkeley

A baby developing in the uterus will have two sets of genes—one set from the mother and one set from the father.

A human baby is created when the mother's egg cell joins with the father's sperm cell. Other living things reproduce by asexual reproduction, which only needs one parent. The offspring of these organisms are exact copies of the parent and each other. They are called clones.

Cloning

Plant clones have been around in nature for millions of years. Some plants, such as strawberries, produce sideways shoots called runners that put down roots and grow into new plants. Others, such as potatoes, develop from underground bulbs. All the new plants are identical to their parents, with exactly the same DNA. In this way, plants can create offspring without needing to join with another plant to reproduce.

Young plants grow into clones—they are identical copies of the parent plant.

Face Facts

"Cloning may be good and it may be bad. Probably it's a bit of both."
Professor Richard Dawkins, Biologist, University of Oxford, United Kingdom

“the debate

Some people question the use of techniques such as tissue cultures to clone plants. They think that people should not interfere with nature. Others argue that plant clones occur in nature anyway, and cloning has many benefits. For example, cloning has produced crops that are resistant to many diseases.”

Scientists create clones of the healthiest crops so that all the plants have the same healthy characteristics.

Creating Healthy Plants

People also produce plant clones on purpose. Gardeners take cuttings of successful, healthy plants and grow them into new plants. The genes that made the parent healthy are then passed on to the new plant. Gardeners cut off a branch of the parent plant, remove the leaves, and plant it in new soil. Over time, new roots develop and the cutting grows into a new plant.

Taking Tissues

Another way of cloning plants is by tissue culture. This involves scraping some material, or tissue, from a parent plant and growing it on a special jelly called agar. The jelly contains nutrients that help the tissue samples to grow into tiny plants, called plantlets. The plantlets are then moved into soil, where they grow into new plants.

Animal Clones

Plants are not the only living things that produce natural clones. The eggs of some animals, such as some insects, fish, frogs, and lizards, can develop into adults without the need for sexual reproduction. The offspring are exact copies of the female that laid the eggs.

Cloning Experiments

In the 1950s, American scientists Robert Briggs and Tom King did an experiment with frog cells. They removed the center, called the nucleus, from a frog cell, so the cell no longer contained DNA. Then they put new DNA from the cell of a frog embryo into this empty egg cell. Eventually, the egg cell developed into a tadpole. However, the tadpole died before it became an adult frog.

The Next Step

In the 1970s, British scientist John Gurdon took the next step in animal cloning. Instead of using the DNA from an embryo, Gurdon used the DNA from an adult frog. The tadpole also died before it became an adult. However, Gurdon's experiment still showed that animal clones could be created from any type of DNA.

Face Facts

"What politicians do not understand is that Wilmut discovered not so much a technical trick as a new law of nature."
Charles Krauthammer, American journalist and doctor

People have created different dog breeds over thousands of years by choosing dogs that have certain traits.

All the bees in a hive are clones of the queen bee. The queen lays eggs that develop into adult bees—without mating with a male bee.

Dolly the Sheep

In 1996, Sir Ian Wilmut and a team of scientists from the Roslin Institute in Edinburgh, Scotland, successfully cloned the first mammal—a sheep named Dolly. The sheep was the first clone created using DNA taken from the cell of an adult animal. Wilmut made more than 275 attempts to create his clone before he was successful. Dolly grew up to become an adult sheep, and even produced four lambs of her own.

ask the experts

In 2003, the team of scientists that cloned Dolly decided to put the animal to sleep. Dolly had diseases common for a sheep twice her age. Professor Richard Gardner, chair of the Royal Society, warned that any link between Dolly's death and the fact she was a clone would "provide further evidence of the dangers inherent in cloning and the irresponsibility of anybody who is trying to extend such work to humans."

These identical twins are natural clones with exactly the same genes.

Face Facts

"The pressures for human cloning are powerful; but, although it seems likely that somebody, at some time, will attempt it, we need not assume that it will ever become a common or significant feature of human life."
Sir Ian Wilmut, University of Edinburgh, Scotland

Human Clones

Since Dolly the sheep, scientists have made many different mammal clones, from cows and pigs, to monkeys and mice. Many scientists now believe that the next step is to clone a special type of mammal—a human being.

Identical Twins

Human clones already exist. These clones are not created in the science lab—they occur naturally every day and all over the world. These natural human clones are identical twins.

Two Babies, Same DNA

Identical twins form after the father's sperm cell joins with the mother's egg cell. The fertilized egg then splits in two. This creates two babies with exactly the same DNA. The twins have a combination of genes from each parent, but they are clones of each other.

Against Nature

There are lots of different opinions about using science to clone people. Some experts argue that human cloning is too risky. They think that human clones may have health problems. Other people have religious objections; they argue that human life is sacred and we should not interfere.

Saving Lives

Other experts support human cloning. They point out that human cloning can be used to create special cells, called stem cells. These cells, which are found in human embryos in the uterus, develop into all the different parts of the body. By taking the stem cells from a cloned embryo, doctors can grow body parts to treat people with diseases.

Scientists extracts stem cells from human embryos for use in medical research.

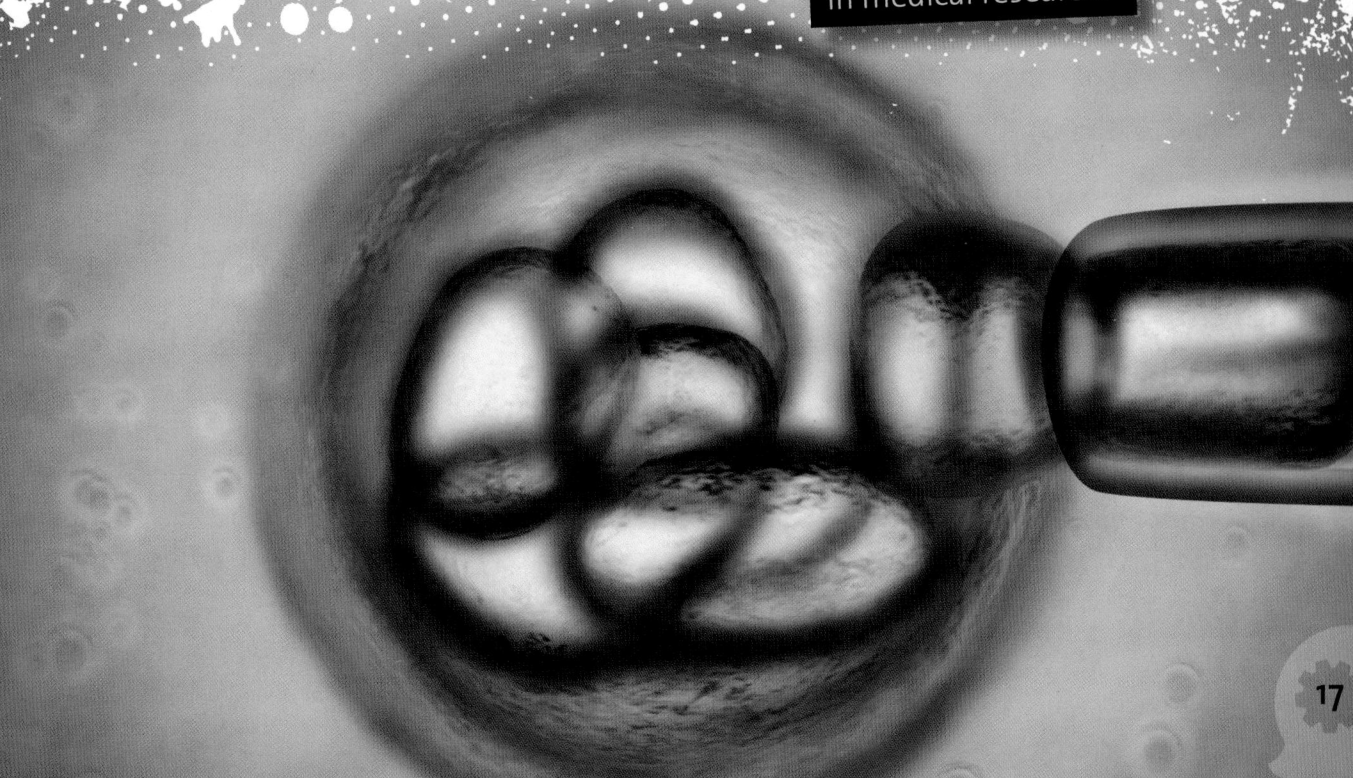

Genetic Modification

For thousands of years, although people did not know about genes, they tried to grow only the healthiest plants and bred only the healthiest animals. Farmers knew that healthy traits would be passed on to the next generation. However, it can take many years and many generations of animals and plants to create new, healthy breeds. GM can speed up this process.

The genetically modified crops grown in fields come from plants created by scientists in the laboratory.

ask the experts

GM does not always mean inserting genes from one animal or plant into another. We can also modify living things by removing, or "switching off," genes to stop something from happening. For example, we can switch off the genes that make fruits go soft as they ripen in the sunlight.

Face Facts

"I see worries in the fact that we have the power to manipulate genes in ways that would be improbable or impossible through conventional evolution. We shouldn't be complacent in thinking that we can predict the results."
Professor Colin Blakemore,
University of Oxford,
United Kingdom

Almost all of the corn grown in the United States has been genetically modified. GM corn is resistant to pests and chemicals called herbicides.

GM or Cloning?

Many people confuse cloning and GM. Cloning and GM use similar scientific methods, but they are not the same. By cloning, scientists create an identical copy of a living thing. That could be a copy of the entire plant or animal, or just one cell of it. They do not alter the copy. In GM, scientists change the DNA of an organism, or even add to it a gene from a different animal or plant.

Why Use GM?

GM allows scientists to create living things with traits they would never have in nature. For example, they can insert a gene into a crop plant, such as corn, to make it resistant to the chemicals farmers use to kill weeds. In fact, food production is one of the main uses of GM. Other uses include scientific research and making medicines.

Scientists have inserted the genes that make this jellyfish glow into other animals. Since the genes cause the glow, scientists can study their effects on the animals' bodies.

GM Organisms

A genetically modified organism (GMO) is any animal, plant, or other living thing that has been changed using the science of GM.

The American scientists Stanley Cohen and Herbert Boyer developed the first GMO in 1973. They chose bacteria, because they are simple organisms. Cohen and Boyer took the DNA from one bacterium and inserted it into the DNA of a different bacterium. Building on their success, the two scientists then inserted the DNA of a frog into the two bacteria cells.

Face Facts

"Natural species are the library from which genetic engineers can work. Genetic engineers don't make new genes, they rearrange existing ones."
Dr. Thomas Lovejoy, Biodiversity Chair of the H. John Heinz III Center for Science, Economics, and the Environment, Washington DC

Plant crops are the most common genetically modified organisms. Scientists are creating new GM crops all the time to help farmers produce more food.

ask the experts

Experts use the word "transgenic" to describe any animal, plant, or other living thing that has been modified with DNA from a different species. So a transgenic organism could be a mouse that has been given DNA from a bacterium or plant. Experts use the word "cisgenic" to describe any GMO that has been modified with DNA from the same species.

GM Animals

The first genetically modified animal was a mouse. German scientist Rudolf Jaenisch created the mouse in 1974, by inserting the gene from a virus into the mouse DNA. Since then, scientists have created genetically modified salmon that grow twice as fast as normal salmon. They have even created cats that glow in the dark!

GM Crops

Since the early days, scientists have created many different GMOs. The most important are plants—crops such as corn and soybeans. GM crops include genes that protect the plants from drought, pesticides, and frost.

At first, people were worried about the use of GM in food, and the technology developed very slowly. Today, although people still have concerns, GM crops are much more common. In the United States alone, the GM food industry is worth around $130 billion a year.

GM takes place in a safe location, such as a laboratory, so that the procedure is carefully controlled. First, scientists prepare the DNA. Next, they insert the DNA into the host to create a GMO. The process requires great skill.

GM in Action

One of the most common methods in GM uses plasmids. These tiny rings of genetic material can be found inside the cells of many bacteria. The plasmid method is therefore useful for modifying bacteria.

"the debate

Many experts worry about using plasmids in GM. They argue that bacteria often exchange plasmids to share genes. So GM bacteria could transfer the genes with other natural bacteria. Other experts say there is nothing to fear. They point out that the GM bacteria are created safely in the lab, and do not come into contact with bacteria in nature."

Scientists inject laboratory mice with GM drugs to find out how a human might react if given the drug.

The scientists involved with GM work in controlled laboratory conditions to ensure their experiments are safe.

Face Facts

"What the world faces is not so much an antibiotic resistance crisis as an epidemic of plasmids."
Professor Thomas O'Brien, Harvard Medical School

Cut and Paste

Scientists isolate the desired gene and then treat the DNA with a special chemical. The chemical cuts the DNA into a tiny strand with "sticky ends." Scientists then take plasmids from the bacteria and add the same chemical. The chemical cuts open the plasmid ring, to create more "sticky ends." The sticky ends of the DNA strand and the plasmid DNA then join up, to form a new ring, which now includes the desired gene.

Inserting the Plasmids

The next stage in the process is to insert the plasmids into new bacteria cells. Fortunately, some bacteria cells will naturally take in the plasmids with the new gene. The GM bacteria then grow and divide as normal.

Viruses

A second popular method in GM is called the vector method. It uses tiny particles called viruses to genetically modify living things. Viruses are packages of DNA that infect cells and cause disease.

The Vector Method

The vector method is almost the same as the plasmid method. Again, scientists use a special chemical to cut the virus DNA and the DNA with the desired gene. The resulting "sticky ends" then join up to form a new virus.

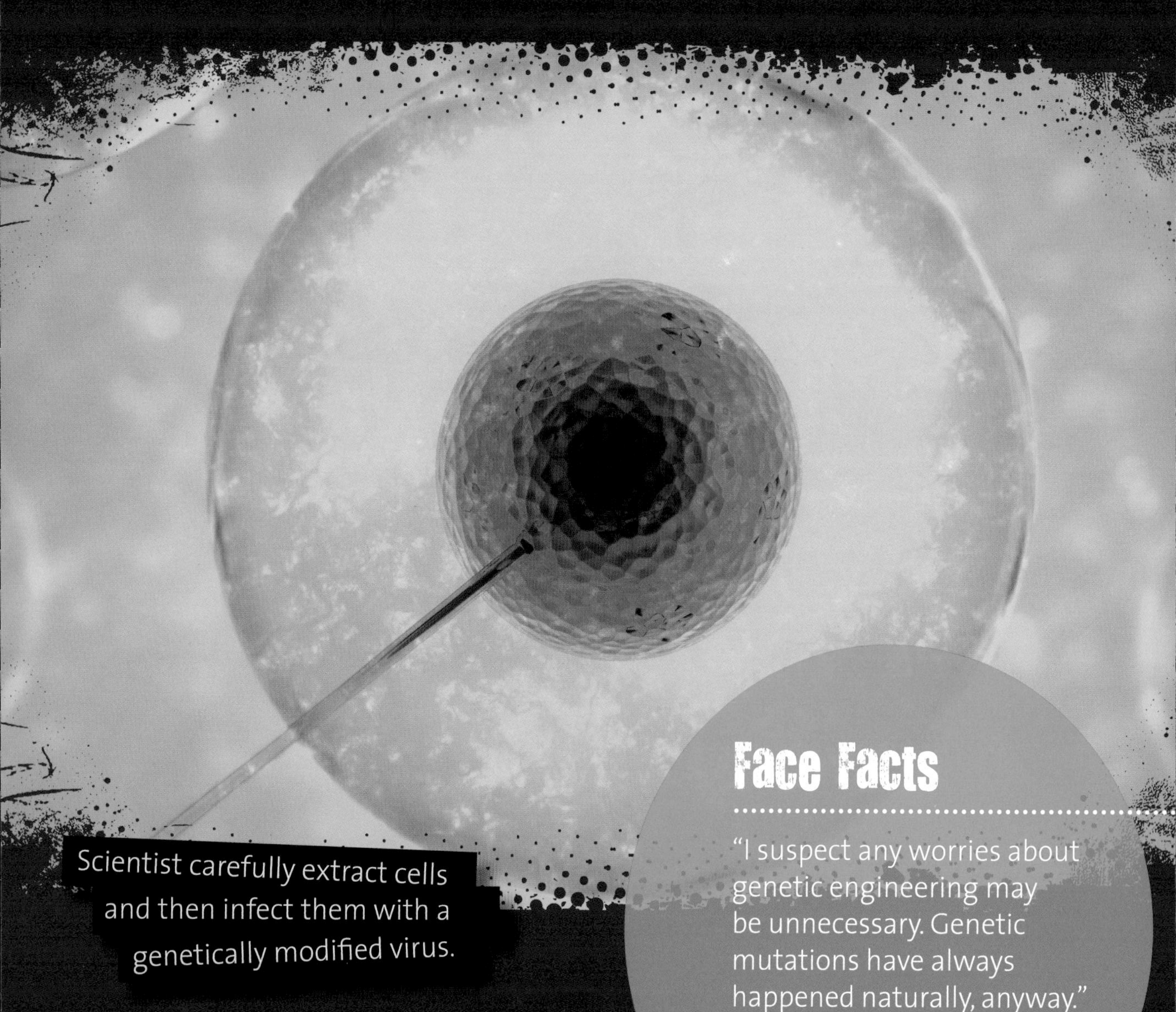

Scientist carefully extract cells and then infect them with a genetically modified virus.

Face Facts

"I suspect any worries about genetic engineering may be unnecessary. Genetic mutations have always happened naturally, anyway." British scientist and environmental expert, James Lovelock

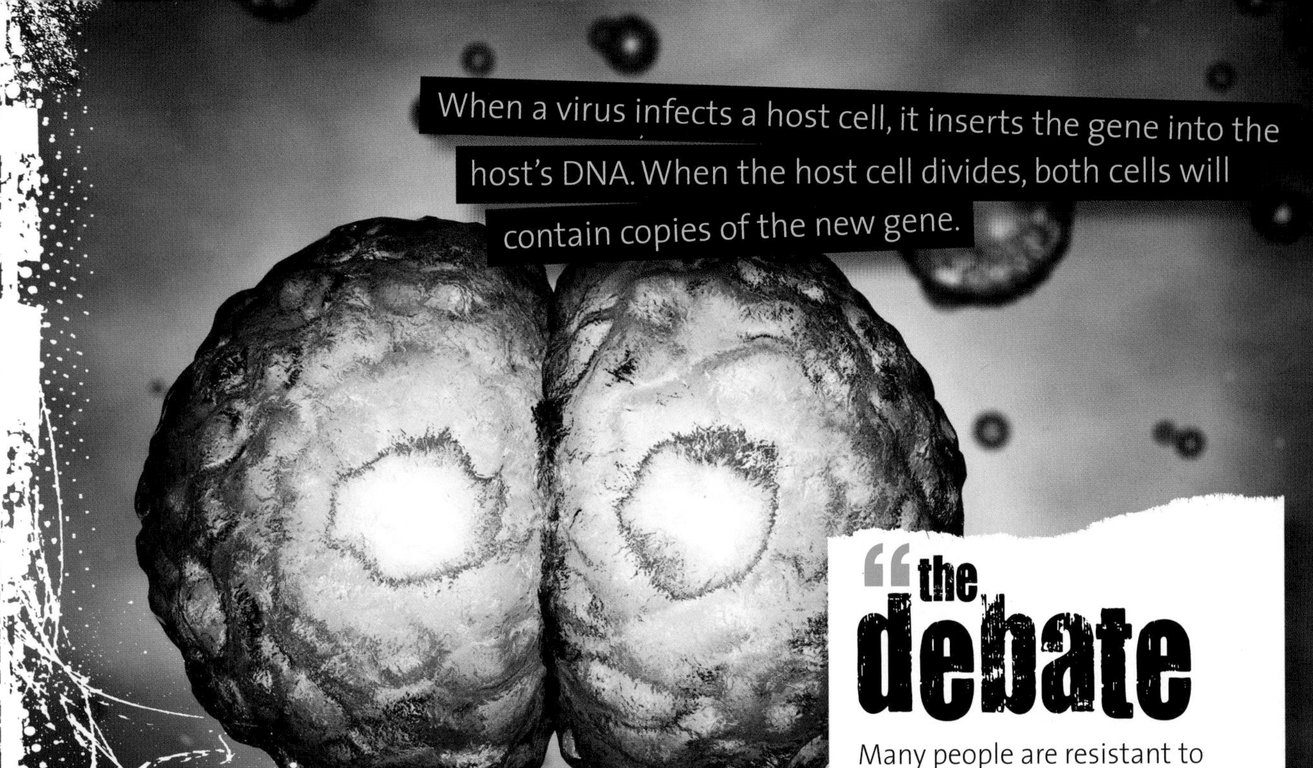

When a virus infects a host cell, it inserts the gene into the host's DNA. When the host cell divides, both cells will contain copies of the new gene.

“the debate

Many people are resistant to using viruses for GM. They believe that it is wrong to deliberately infect living things with viruses—even if the virus has been made safe. Others argue that doctors have been using these safe, inactive viruses to vaccinate people against diseases for many years, without any problems.”

Safety First

What makes viruses ideal for GM is that they infect cells naturally. As a result, there is a good chance the host organism will take up the new DNA. However, this also raises a problem—the same virus could make the host ill. Scientists must first take out the portion of the virus DNA that causes the symptoms of the illness, so that the viruses can be used safely.

Infecting the Host

Once the virus DNA is made safe, scientists use it to infect a host. This could be a bacterium, or it could be a plant or an animal. When the virus infects the cells, it transfers DNA to the host, including the desired gene. The GMO is then ready to use.

GM Gunning

Scientists sometimes use “gene guns” to genetically modify plants. They use the guns to fire tiny metal pellets at plant cells. The pellets are coated with DNA containing the desired gene. Some of the plant cells take up the DNA, and then grow into new plants. Scientist can then clone the plants to create a crop of genetically identical organisms.

GM in Food

The world's population is increasing rapidly. Many people worry that in years to come there will be a huge shortage of food. They fear that farmers will struggle to grow enough crops to feed everyone in the world. Genetic modification can offer some solutions to this problem.

Farmers are running out of land on which to grow enough food for the world's rising population.

ask the experts

In 2011, Professor Sir John Beddington, Chief Scientific Advisor for the United Kingdom government, summarized the global food crisis in an interview with the BBC: "There is an enormously serious problem of feeding the world in the future, in the face of problems such as climate change, population growth, and energy shortages. If there are genetically modified (GM) organisms that actually solve problems... then we should use them."

Face Facts

"The poor and hungry need low-cost, readily available technologies and practices to increase food production."
New Scientist, 2001

Refugee camps fill with hungry people during times of famine. Many people hope that GM will solve the world's food crisis.

Population Pressure

Experts suggest that if the world's population continues to grow at its current rate, by 2030 there will not be enough food for everyone on the planet. They think that there is an urgent need to produce more food so people will not starve. The obvious answer is to grow more food, but we are running out of land on which to grow it. Today, more than 12 percent of our planet is used to grow crops. Farmers are cutting down rain forests, and other natural habitats to make way for cultivating crops. There is not much land left on which to grow more food in the future.

Eat Less, Waste Less

Another solution to the problem is for people in some parts of the world to consume less and waste less of the food resources we currently have. This is important in rich countries such as the United States, United Kingdom, and the countries of Europe, where people are throwing away millions of tons of food every day. Most people in these developed countries are also consuming more food than they need.

GM Food

Some experts think that GM is the answer to the world's food crisis. They believe that GM can help in two ways. First, it can improve the yields from crops, for example, by making them resistant to disease and pesticides. Second, it can create bigger animals. Both things will result in more food for people worldwide to eat.

Scientists have created GM animals such as pigs. As yet, no countries have approved GM animals for use as human food.

Face Facts

"From a scientific perspective, the public argument about genetically modified organisms, I think, will soon be a thing of the past. The science has moved on and we're now in the genomics era."
Professor Bob Goodman, former head of research and development at Calgene

GM on the Table

GM foods have been around since the 1990s. Scientists have developed GM crops to protect them from being destroyed by insects and other pests. Other GM crops are modified so they are resistant to chemicals called herbicides. This means that farmers can kill the weeds that harm crops in the fields without damaging their valuable crops.

Flavr Savr Tomatoes

The Flavr Savr tomato was the first commercially grown GM food. An American company called Calgene created the tomato in the late 1980s. It wanted to make a tomato that kept fresher for longer. Scientists at the company added a gene to the plants that slowed the ripening process. This stopped the tomatoes from going soft

Modified Crops

Today, many different GM crops are grown around the world. They include important crops such as corn and soybeans. The world's biggest grower is the United States. Every year, American farmers grow hundreds of millions of tons of GM crops, and this figure keeps on rising year after year.

Modified Animals

Scientists are now looking to modify animals for food. In 2010, scientists in the United States created a genetically modified salmon that grows much bigger than a normal salmon. They wanted to create bigger fish so they could feed more people. Scientists in China have also genetically modified animals for food. In 2011, they inserted genes into dairy cows to make the animals produce human breast milk. In the future, human mothers may be able to feed their babies with this new milk, instead of using "formula" milk.

ask the experts

Farmers have grown GM crops in the United States since 2000 without any major health concerns. It has taken much longer for countries in Europe to accept GM crops. Why? Many experts think that newspapers are to blame. Journalists have given GM crops names such as "Franken-foods." This scares people into thinking GM crops are dangerous.

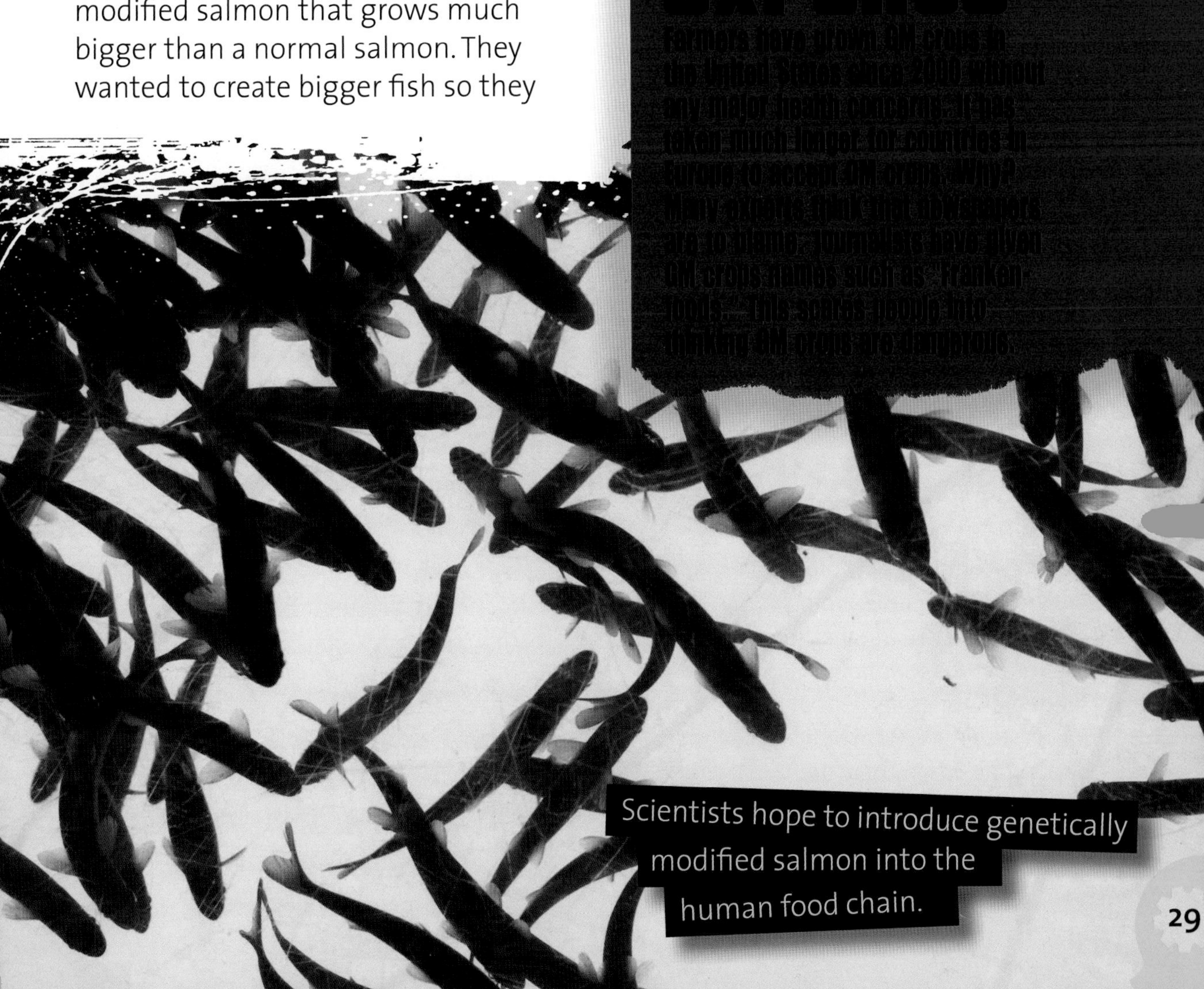

Scientists hope to introduce genetically modified salmon into the human food chain.

The Food Debate

It looks like GM crops are here to stay. More farmers in more countries are growing GM crops, and they are now found in many different foods. Now scientists hope to put GM animals into the human food chain. This has put the GM food debate back in the spotlight.

GM Food—the Benefits

GM has many benefits. Farmers need to spray their crops with herbicides and pesticides to protect them from weeds and pests. These chemicals may save the crops, but they harm the environment. GM crops have genes to protect them from pests and disease. This means farmers can spray fewer chemicals on their crops, saving both money and the environment.

Beating the Weather

Scientists have also developed GM crops that grow even when it is cold and frosty, or when there is not much water. Normally, crops would die in these conditions. This has opened up new areas of land for farming, where it would not otherwise be possible. This means far more food can be produced.

In the future, farmers may be able to grow GM crops in areas where there is little rainfall.

"the debate

Many people think that food companies should label foods to say they contain GM ingredients. They say that people should have a choice about whether they eat foods containing GM products. Others argue that labels suggest GM foods are dangerous, when there are no proven health risks."

GM Food—the Concerns

One of the main concerns about GM crops is the damage they could do to the planet. Some people think that the genes in GM crops could spread to other plants in the wild. For example, the genes that give GM crops resistance to pesticides could spread to wild plants, resulting in new "superweeds." Another concern is the risk to human health. Since GM uses bacteria and viruses, many people believe that eating GM foods might create new diseases. GM crops have only been around since 2000. Who knows what the effects of eating them will be 10 years from now?

Face Facts

"With genetically modified foods I believe we have reached the thin edge of the wedge, we are messing with the building blocks of life and it's scary."
Malcolm Walker, Chairman and Chief Executive of Iceland Foods

Right now, millions of people around the world are starving. Many people think that GM food is the only way to solve the global food crisis.

GM has many important uses in medicine. Scientists already use GM to make drugs and vaccines to treat and prevent diseases. Doctors are using GM animals to learn more about human diseases. Gene therapy is a new and exciting development. However, many people are concerned about the use of GM in medicine.

GM Medicine

Face Facts

"The new science of genetic engineering aims to take a dramatic shortcut in the slow process of evolution."
Brian Stableford, biologist and author

Vaccinations save millions of lives every year by preventing deadly diseases such as polio and smallpox.

Genetic modification has been used to create many drugs that doctors need to treat diseases. Today, genetically modified bacteria make most of these drugs. GM bacteria are used to mass-produce insulin, for example, which is used to treat a disease called diabetes (see pages 34–35). In the future, scientists hope to create GM animals, such as cows and goats, which will deliver medicines in their milk.

Making Vaccines

Another use of GM is to create vaccines. Vaccination involves injecting people with weak forms of a virus that causes a disease. The body's immune system then builds up a natural protection against the disease. Scientists use GM methods to make the viruses safe, so the vaccine does not make people ill.

Curing Cancer

Scientists hope to use GM to create monoclonal antibodies, to treat serious diseases such as cancer. Monoclonal antibodies are tiny particles that target cancer cells in the human body. Scientists make them by injecting human cancer cells into mice. Cells in the mouse's body encourage antibodies to fight the cancer. Scientists remove these cells and join them with human cells. Doctors can then use these joined-up cells to treat the cancer.

ask the experts

Scientists think they are getting closer to being able to change the DNA of mosquitoes, to stop the spread of a deadly disease called malaria. This disease kills millions of people every year, many of them children. Only female mosquitoes spread malaria, when they feed on human blood. So scientists are considering inserting genes into adult mosquitoes to make them produce only male offspring.

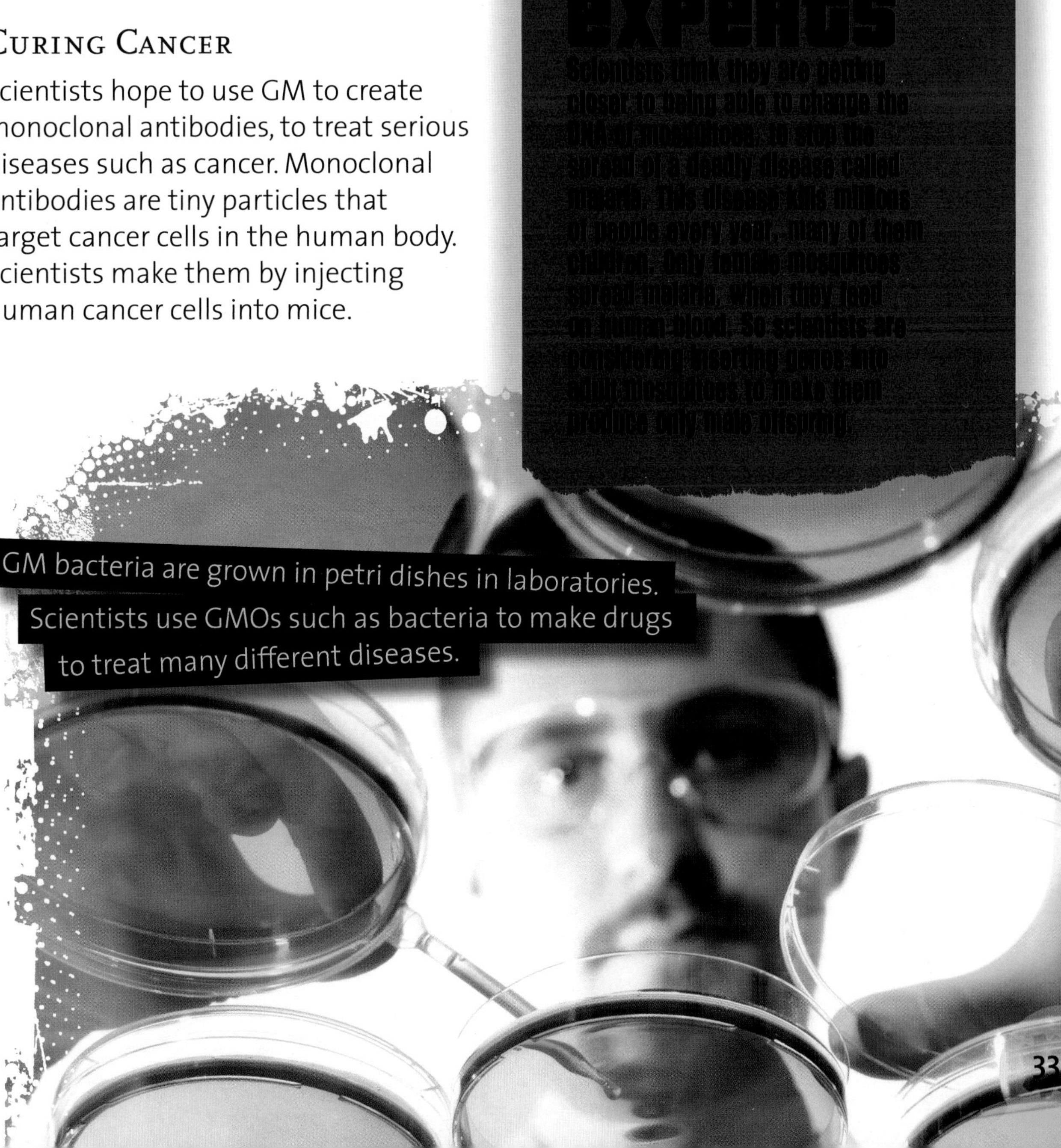

GM bacteria are grown in petri dishes in laboratories. Scientists use GMOs such as bacteria to make drugs to treat many different diseases.

What Is Insulin?

Insulin is a substance that controls the level of sugar in a person's blood. When a person eats, his or her body converts the food into sugar, and the body releases insulin. The insulin ensures that the blood delivers the sugar to all the cells in the body so they can work properly.

Producing Insulin

Insulin was the first medicine to be produced by GM. American scientist Herbert Boyer made it in the laboratory in 1977 by genetically modifying a bacterium called *E. coli*. Five years later, the insulin was ready for medical use.

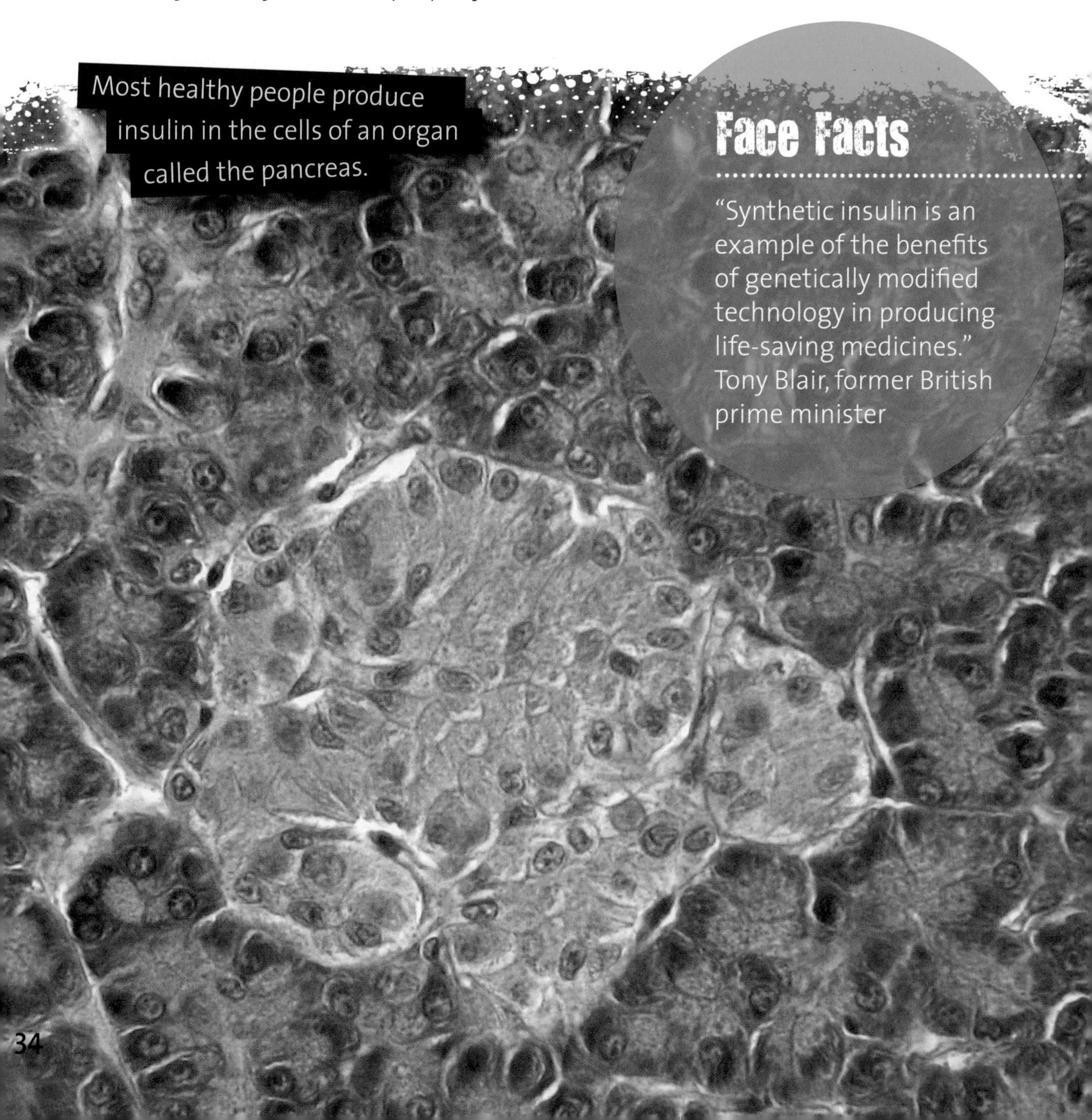

Most healthy people produce insulin in the cells of an organ called the pancreas.

Face Facts

"Synthetic insulin is an example of the benefits of genetically modified technology in producing life-saving medicines."
Tony Blair, former British prime minister

A diabetic must test the level of sugar in her blood regularly.

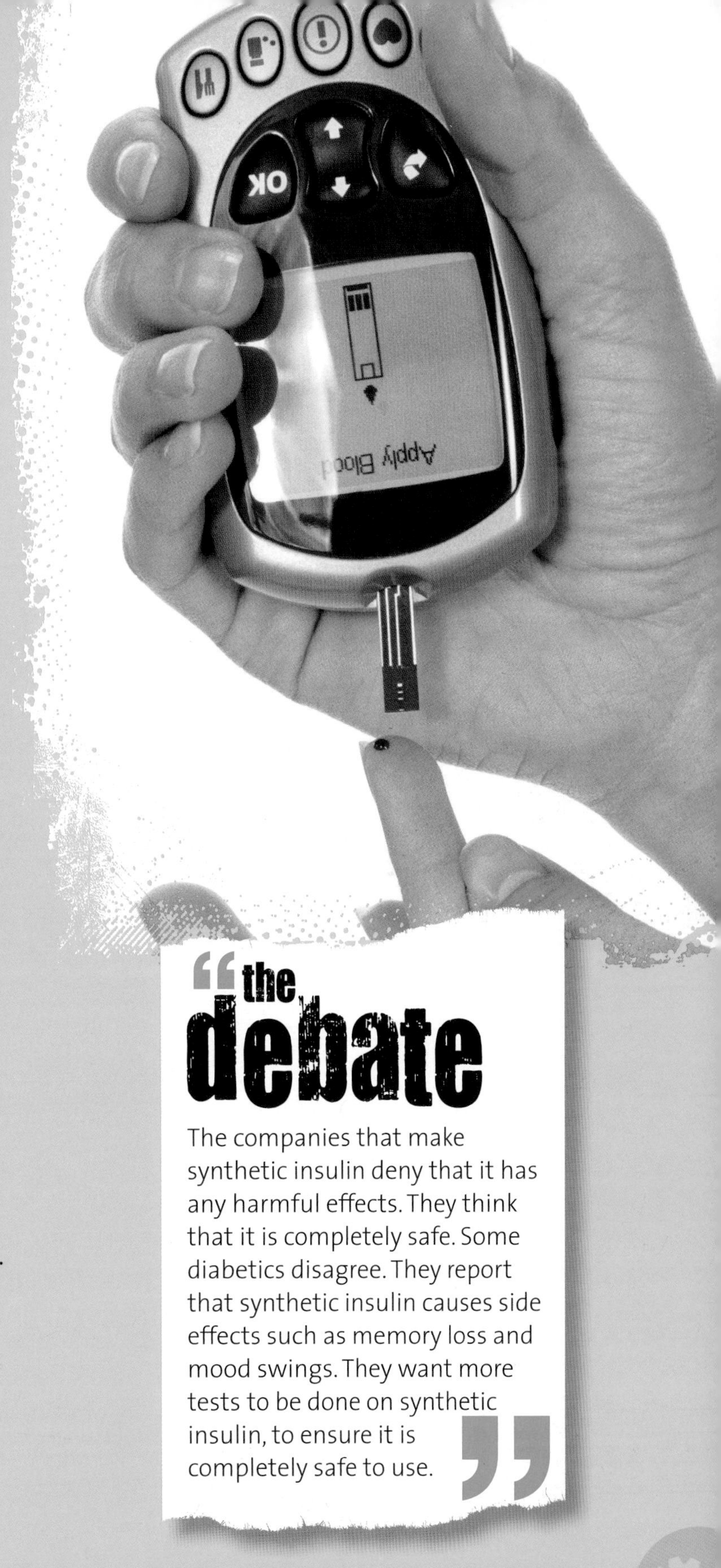

Diabetes

Some people have a disease called diabetes. They are called diabetics. A diabetic cannot naturally produce enough insulin, so the sugar from food cannot reach their body's cells. Instead, it builds up in the blood. Without sugar, the cells slowly starve. Eventually, the diabetic will die. As a result, diabetics need to take in insulin by injecting it every day, to keep their blood sugar levels in check.

Synthetic Insulin

Before GM, diabetics injected the insulin produced by animals such as dogs and pigs. Then, Herbert Boyer used GM to make synthetic insulin in his laboratory. He inserted the human gene for insulin into the DNA of bacteria called *E. coli*. The bacteria started making the insulin. As the bacteria divided, they produced more and more insulin. Today, most diabetics use insulin that has been produced in this way.

"the debate

The companies that make synthetic insulin deny that it has any harmful effects. They think that it is completely safe. Some diabetics disagree. They report that synthetic insulin causes side effects such as memory loss and mood swings. They want more tests to be done on synthetic insulin, to ensure it is completely safe to use."

Face Facts

"Research on animals has contributed to almost every medical advance of the last century."
United Kingdom Department of Health, 2001

Scientists rely on laboratory animals such as rats for medical research.

Animal Experiments

Scientists commonly use GM animals for medical research. They are creating animal experiments to study many human diseases, ranging from cancer and dementia to heart disease.

Medical Mouse

The mouse is by far the most common GM animal used to study human diseases. One example is the oncomouse. Scientists from Harvard University in the United States created the oncomouse in 1984. They injected laboratory mice with a gene that made them more likely to develop cancer. Today, the oncomouse is commonly used worldwide for cancer research.

GM, Disease, and Aging

Scientists have used other GM mice to study many other diseases, ranging from diabetes to obesity. They have even used the mice to study natural processes, such as aging, in the hope of slowing it

Organ Transplants

Scientists are also turning to GM to provide organs for human transplants. Today, doctors need healthy organs, such as kidneys and hearts, to save lives. Many sick patients are dying in hospitals while waiting for transplants, because there are not enough healthy organs to go around.

Growing New Organs

Scientists hope that GM pigs and other animals could provide a new supply of vital organs for human transplants. Scientists modify the pig organ by injecting it with genes from the patient waiting for the transplant. The genes produce chemicals that coat the organ with human cells.

Limiting Rejection

Surgeons can then transplant the organ into the patient's body. Since the organ is covered with the patient's own cells, the body is much less likely to reject it.

"the debate

There are many arguments for and against using animals for medical research. Some people think that human life is worth more than animal life. Humans kill animals every day for food. Why is medical research any different? Other people think that animals have just as much right to life as humans. Animals suffer in in laboratories. Can we be sure they do not feel pain?"

Animal rights campaigners protest against the use of animals for scientific research. Many people believe animals have the same rights as human beings.

Gene therapy could be used for the wrong reasons. Parents could use it to create "designer babies" with particular features such as hair or skin color.

Unlocking Secrets

As scientists unlock the secrets of the human genome, they are finding more genes and more genetically-linked diseases. They hope that new developments in GM will help to solve our health issues, many of which are passed from parent to child. One solution is gene therapy.

What Is Gene Therapy?

Gene therapy builds on the tried and tested methods of genetic modification. It involves inserting genes into a person's DNA, either to replace absent or faulty genes, or to provide genes the body can use to fight disease. Scientists usually use viruses to insert the desired gene into the patient's DNA.

"the debate

Many people are worried about using gene therapy. They believe people will use the technology for the wrong reasons. For example, parents could use gene therapy to create "designer babies"—picking out genetic features such as height and hair color to choose what their children might look like. Others say gene therapy could prevent diseases passing from parent to child."

Different Types of Therapy

There are two types of gene therapy. The first type involves transferring genes into cells called somatic cells—these are all the normal cells that make up your body. For this reason, it is called somatic gene therapy. This type of gene therapy can treat an individual patient, but his or her children may still develop the genetically transmitted disease.

The second type of therapy involves transferring genes into the sex cells—the male sperm or the female eggs. When they are combined, these cells develop into a healthy person, who, in turn, can then pass on their healthy genes to his or her children.

Curing Diseases

Gene therapy is still in its early stages, and has only been used in medical trials. Even so, doctors have used gene therapy to treat many different diseases, including blood disorders and cancers. Animal experiments have also been promising—animal gene therapy has cured blindness and deafness.

Many people with disabilities lead normal lives. Should we use gene therapy to prevent the genetic conditions that cause disabilities?

Face Facts

"Over the next 20 to 30 years, gene therapy will probably revolutionize the practice of medicine."
Dr. W. French Anderson, director of The Gene Therapy Laboratories at the University of Southern California

Genetic modification is a vital tool in science and industry. Scientists use GM methods to experiment with genes and find out how they work. GM is also important in industry. As well as helping to produce food and medicine, GM has been used to clean up pollution and create works of "biological art."

Science and Industry

Research scientists have used GM to create novelty pets such as glow-in-the-dark fish.

Face Facts

"Mice must not become mere research tools, sheep mere bioreactors, nor pigs spare-part factories."
Dr. Donald Bruce, Chair of the Church of Scotland's Society, Religion, and Technology Project

Biological Factories

GMOs are biological factories. Scientists now use bacteria, viruses, and other living things to create many different products, from drugs and food to vaccines and fuel.

GM bacteria are now used to clean up after oil spills. Other bacteria contain genes to break down other toxic waste products.

Oil Spills

Another important industrial use for GMOs is clearing up dangerous waste products. For example, scientists have created GM bacteria to "feed" on oil. In 2010, scientists used these oil-eating GM bacteria to help clean up a giant oil spill. The spill followed an enormous explosion on the Deepwater Horizon oil platform in the Gulf of Mexico.

"the debate"

Many experts believe that the oil-eating GM bacteria that were used to clean up the oil spill in the Gulf of Mexico are spreading across the world's oceans. They think these bacteria are unsafe, and may even be destroying animals that live in the ocean.

"Enviropig"

Scientists have also created GM pigs to help keep the planet clean. Like all animals, pigs need an element called phosphorus to stay healthy. But the pigs find it hard to digest phosphorus in their food. Most of it comes out in the pig's waste. This washes into rivers and lakes, and feeds bacteria and plants called algae. When the many algae die, they fuel bacteria which uses up all the oxygen in the water, killing living things such as fish. Scientists in Canada created the "Enviropig" to solve this problem. This pig has a gene that makes a protein to break down the phosphorus in its food, thus reducing the pollution problem.

Other Uses

GM has many other uses in industry. For example, scientists have created GM bacteria to make batteries that cause less damage to the environment. They are also using the technology to create "Bioart," and novelty animals and plants that glow in the dark.

Scientific Research

GM is an important tool for scientists. They use GMOs to find out what genes do, and how they work. Scientists use four key methods to study genes and their effects, as follows:

Loss-of-Function Studies

These experiments are known as "knockout" studies, because scientists "knock out" one or more genes in the DNA of the organism, to make the genes inactive. By comparing the differences between an organism with an active gene and one with an inactive gene, scientists can learn more about what the gene does within the body.

Gain-of-Function Studies

The opposite of knockout studies, gain-of-function studies are tests in which scientists add extra copies of the same gene to the DNA of an organism. This increases the function of the gene. In this way, scientists can study the effects of the gene more easily.

ask the experts

Some experts believe that we are not far away from creating the first human-made organisms that do not occur in nature. This is known as synthetic biology. Many people object to the creation of artificial life. They believe that scientists should not "play God" with nature.

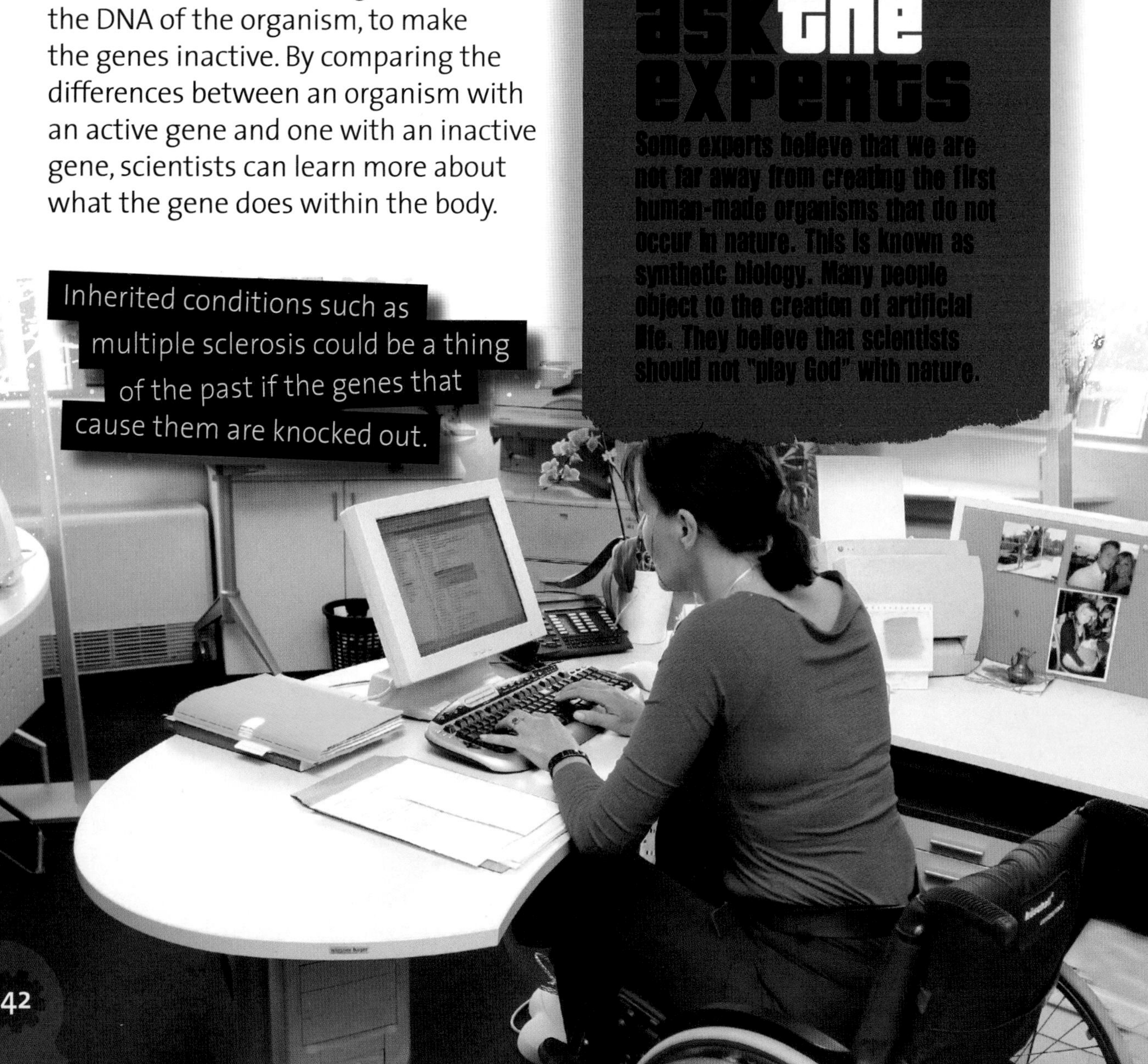

Inherited conditions such as multiple sclerosis could be a thing of the past if the genes that cause them are knocked out.

Tracking Studies

Some studies help scientists to study how and where genes act on the body of an organism. Scientists modify the genes they want to study with genes that make special glowing proteins, such as green fluorescent protein. The glowing proteins reveal exactly where in the body of the organism the gene is having an effect.

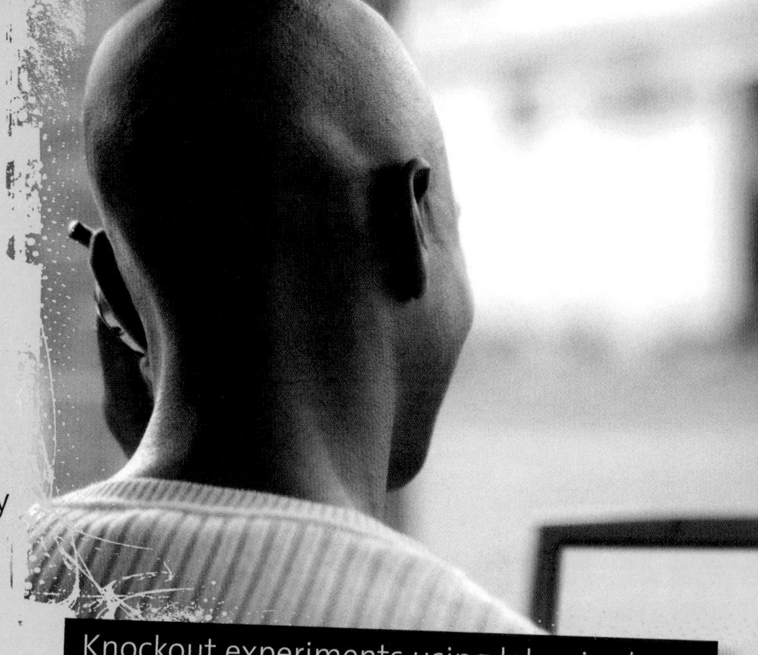

Knockout experiments using lab mice have been used to study the genes that control hair growth.

Expression Studies

These experiments help scientists find out where and when genes make proteins in the body of an organism. Scientists use glowing proteins to reveal where and when a particular protein is made.

Face Facts

"We have to devote the necessary resources to scientific and technological research and development, including biotechnology." Thabo Mbeki, South African politician

Scientific research is vital to understanding the full consequences of genetic modification.

Genetic modification is a new science, but it has already changed our lives beyond our wildest imaginations. As the genetic revolution continues to march on, do you think it is just moving too quickly? Do you believe that this new technology is making life easier, or do you believe it is putting our lives and world at risk?

You're the Expert

Do you think scientists are "playing God" by interfering with the natural processes that go on inside cells?

ask the experts

Experts agree that it is probably too late to stop GM. It now plays a vital role in producing enough food for us to eat, medicines to cure diseases, and it could lead to other solutions yet undiscovered. Who knows how else we will genetically modify our world in the future?

Force for Good

Do you believe the convincing arguments that GM is changing our lives for the better? Supporters suggest that it is solving the world's food crisis. GM crops now provide a reliable source of food for the world's ever-increasing population. GM saves lives by providing medicines in the fight against disease.

Force for Bad

Maybe you are not convinced that GM is the way forward? Do you think that scientists should not interfere with nature without understanding the full consequences of their actions? Perhaps we simply do not know enough about GM to be sure it is completely safe, and more research needs to be done into its effects. If you were the expert, what would you decide?

Face Facts

"We used to think that our fate was in our stars, but now we know that, in large measure, our fate is in our genes."
James Watson, biologist and DNA pioneer

GM will change the lives of millions of people around the world if it can be used to solve the problems of famine and disease.

Glossary

allele a different form of the same gene; for example, there is an allele for blond hair color and an allele for brown hair color

bacterium a single-celled living organism. Some bacteria are useful, while others cause disease.

DNA short for deoxyribonucleic acid, a substance found in the nucleus of most cells. DNA carries the genetic code for almost all living things.

cancer a disease caused by the rapid growth of cells in part of the body

cells the building blocks of all living things

chromosome a tightly-packed, threadlike molecule of DNA

cisgenic organism any animal, plant, or other living thing that has been modified with DNA from the same species

clone an organism that is an exact copy of its parent

diabetes a disease caused by the lack of a chemical in the body called insulin

egg a female sex cell

embryo an animal or plant in its earliest stages of development

gene the sequences of DNA that determine the characteristics of living organisms. Genes are passed from parents to their children

genome the complete set of genes in the cell of a living thing

herbicide a chemical used to kill weeds

immune system the system in the body that protects it from disease

insulin a chemical that controls the amount of sugar in the blood

malaria a disease caused by a tiny organism that lives in mosquitoes. It passes into the human body when the mosquitoes feed on blood.

nucleus the center of a cell that contains almost all of an organism's DNA

nutrient a substance that living things need to grow and stay healthy

obesity the condition of being extremely overweight

pesticide a chemical used to kill pests such as some insects

plasmids tiny rings of genetic material found inside the cells of many bacteria

proteins substances in cells that control all the different life processes in the body

species the same kind of living thing that can breed and produce offspring

sperm a male sex cell

transgenic organism any animal, plant, or other living thing that has been modified with DNA from a different species

vaccine a weak form of a virus that is injected into the body to build up natural protection against a disease

virus a tiny package of DNA that infects cells and cause diseases

Books

Cohen, Marina. *Let's Relate to Genetics: Genetic Engineering.* New York, NY: Crabtree Publishing, 2009.

Moore, Pete. *Ethical Debates: Genetic Engineering.* London: Hodder Wayland, 2010.

Morgan, Sally. *Science at the Edge: Body Doubles: Cloning Plants and Animals.* Chicago: Heinemann Raintree, 2009.

For More Information

Websites

Visit the University of Utah's Learn.Genetics™ website to find out how genetics affects our lives. There are lots of activities, labs, experiments, and workshops at:
http://learn.genetics.utah.edu

Visit Tiki the Penguin's website for an excellent guide to genetic engineering:
http://tiki.oneworld.net/genetics/GE6.html

Visit the American Museum of Natural History to go on a genetic journey, find out what makes you special, get the scoop on DNA and cloning, and much more:
www.ology.amnh.org/genetics

Publisher's note to educators and parents: Our editors have carefully reviewed these websites to ensure that they are suitable for students. Many websites change frequently, however, and we cannot guarantee that a site's future contents will continue to meet our high standards of quality and educational value. Be advised that students should be closely supervised whenever they access the Internet.

Index